THE MIGRANT FARMWORKER'S SON

A Play in Two Acts
by
SILVIA GONZALEZ S.

Dramatic Publishing
Woodstock, Illinois • London, England • Melbourne, Australia

∴ NOTICE ***

The amateur and stock acting rights to this work are controlled exclusively by THE DRAMATIC PUBLISHING COMPANY without whose permission in writing no performance of it may be given. Royalty fees are given in our current catalogue and are subject to change without notice. Royalty must be paid every time a play is performed whether or not it is presented for profit and whether or not admission is charged. A play is performed any time it is acted before an audience. All inquiries concerning amateur and stock rights should be addressed to:

DRAMATIC PUBLISHING
P. O. Box 129, Woodstock, Illinois 60098.

THE MIGRANT FARMWORKER'S SON

A Play in Two Acts
For 3 Men and 2 Women, 3-5 peasants

CHARACTERS

HENRY .... high school student, Hispanic
OLIVERIO SANTOS .... a farmworker, Mexican-American
DAD .... Mexican national, thirties
MOM .... Mexican national, thirties
GIRL .... Mexican-American, six to eight years old
BLUE MEXICAN PEASANTS (3-5)

PLACE: A rural community in Yuma, Arizona.

TIME: 1970-1985.

SCENES

ACT ONE
Scene One: 1970
Scene Two: 1972
Scene Three: 1985 (early rap days)
Scene Four: Late that evening
Scene Five: Next day
Scene Six: Late at night
Scene Seven: Next day
Scene Eight: Two days later
Scene Nine: Later that day
Scene Ten: Same day
Scene Eleven: Same day
Scene Twelve: Next day
Scene Thirteen: A few days later
Scene Fourteen: Next day

ACT TWO
Scene One: Three months later
Scene Two: Same day
Scene Three: That evening
Scene Four: Next day
Scene Five: That evening
Scene Six: Same evening
Scene Seven: Two months later
Scene Eight: That evening

ACT ONE

SCENE ONE

*(Eerie blue light. Sounds of a tractor going across a field.
Silhouette light, chest up, on OLIVERIO looking blankly
out. BLUE MEXICAN PEASANTS cut lettuce off the
ground and bag them. [This is like a dance.] MOM and
DAD also work the ground. [They are younger.] After a
few moments, rough sounds from a tractor trying to stop in
the distance are heard. Lights dim out on OLIVERIO. The
PEASANTS look in the opposite direction. In awe, MOM
and DAD and the PEASANTS start to move towards the
sound, then stop. Sounds of a tractor, losing control, fol-
lowed by music.)*

BLUE MEXICAN PEASANT *(religious). Aye, Dios mio.*
*(The MEN take off their hats and the WOMEN cover their
heads with their rebozos and turn away sadly. Eerie light.
Slow blackout.)*

SCENE TWO

*(A young GIRL enters in a ruffled dress and hair in braids.
She is playful and full of charm. The light is slightly on
her. Purple shadows behind her. She is talking to a baby in
a crib, but it is not seen.)*

GIRL. Bay-bee. Leetle bay-bee. Cahm here, leetle baby.
That's how Mommy called you...I'm going to sing you a

5

little song. Itzy bitzy spider, went up the water spout. Down came the rain and...But, Daddy, I learned the song in school. Down came the rain and washed the spider out...Daddy, I like to...It's pretty...Out came the sun and...(*Long pause.*) Don't, Daddy, please.

SCENE THREE

(*DAD enters with a crate of oranges. He's wearing field clothes and is quite weathered. He puts the crate aside. Then exits and enters with a Nintendo game. He sets it up to play. MOM enters. She has already changed from working in the fields. She has a nice clean appearance. She is drying her hair.*)

MOM. What's that?

DAD. Nintendo.

MOM. Where's the telephone? What did I say to do after work?

DAD. It's for Enrigue.

MOM. *Henry*?

DAD. *Enrigue*. His name is Enrigue. You keep forgetting your own son's name.

MOM. What about the telephone?

DAD. Look how they put a game in the TV and you can play. Right here on the sofa. It's new. Everybody is getting one.

MOM. How much did that cost?

DAD. Practically nothing. Beto had to get rid of it. He was getting too addicted to it. It was taking all his beer time. We all forced him to sell it to me.

MOM. So the money is gone? Last time you were supposed to get a new carburetor, and instead, you gave the money to your brother.

DAD. He needed it to pay rent.

MOM. Does he ever return favors?

DAD *(looks at her with extreme sadness, returns to game).* He did one time. *(Long moment.)*

MOM *(softly).* Play your game.

DAD *(recuperating well).* They say Mario is Italian, but I think he's a Mexicano. *(Pause.)* Aye, Mario hit a wall.

(HENRY enters with headphones. HENRY is much like a boy of today, in manner and dress. The clash of the cultures is obvious. HENRY will attempt to make lighter many moments until a certain point.)

HENRY. Wow! Dad bought a Nintendo. All right! Give me the controls.

DAD. No. *Todavia* no. *(MOM exits.)*

HENRY. Hey, Mom? What's the matter with her?

DAD. Ah! She's mad at me.

HENRY. For what?

DAD. Nothing. Women.

HENRY. Yeah, women.

DAD. Don't let a woman work. She'll think she's wearing the pants in the house.

MOM *(off).* I do. And I'm a harder worker than you in the fields.

DAD. You are working there because you want to. If we lived in Mexico, they would shame me for letting her work. A real man doesn't allow that.

HENRY. Then why do you cook, Dad?

DAD. Sh! That's a family secret. Never tell anyone what goes on in this house. Understand? I told you that before. It's not the way. *(Back to Nintendo.)* Look at that funny guy. He's a cartoon.

(MOM enters with a basket of clothes.)

MOM. You're a cartoon.

DAD. She wouldn't talk like that to me if we lived over there. And *your* Spanish would be better. *(Pause.)* I'm ready to go tomorrow to get my dignity back.

MOM. They already stepped on it and tossed it out into the gutter. You know I am not going back. And you're not going back either. You're dad's been talking like this for fifteen years. *(HENRY hasn't been listening. He is wearing his Walkman.)*

DAD. Are you making fun of me?

MOM. You're not going back. You would die of starvation over there.

DAD. I don't believe it.

MOM. I do. Why do you think you're here?

DAD. There's death in this dirt. *(MOM turns away. HENRY looks as if he is used to this situation, even though he's not sure what they are talking about. There is silence for awhile.)*

MOM. Henry wouldn't make it over there. And why should I go back?

DAD. Is there another man?

MOM. What?

DAD. Do you have a man to take care of you already?

MOM. No. You don't need a man in the United States.

DAD *(to HENRY)*. See that. She's becoming more *gringa* every day. *(HENRY's not listening. DAD knocks HENRY's headphones off.)* Want to go with me to Mexico?

HENRY. Of course not.

DAD. Why not?

HENRY. Like you said, I don't speak Spanish well.

DAD. You used to speak Spanish when you were a child. Why did she have it in her head you would do better in life with only English? Now look at you. You don't understand half the things I say. This is a conspiracy to take you away from me and from the mother country.

HENRY. Dad, I like everything the way it is.

DAD. Ah! What do you know?

MOM. I'm his mother and I look after his education.

DAD. You took my son away. *(Silence.)*

HENRY. I'm not like you, Dad. We're different. Sorry.

MOM. That's not what's bothering him. You don't like it that I am learning too.

DAD. *Basta.*

MOM. I like to learn.

DAD. It's a waste of time for a woman to learn.

HENRY. Dad, you got to stop living in the stone age.

DAD. *¿Que?*

HENRY. Let her be. *(DAD looks at HENRY with inexplicable rage. He often does this.)*

MOM. Go, Henry. I'll take care of this.

DAD. Come here, *pocho.** (DAD motions for HENRY to approach. DAD touches his belt as a threat to HENRY, but MOM doesn't see this action.)*

HENRY. We live in America, Dad. You can't do that.

DAD. You must respect your father.

* *Slang term for being neither Mexican, nor American.*

HENRY. Who is going to respect me? *(MOM directs HENRY out to get DAD a beer. MOM stares at DAD.)*

DAD *(softening)*. I did the same to my father. He is growing up.

MOM. And what did he do?

DAD. Enrigue's very first words, between the tears and pooping in his pants, were *"Hola papá."*

MOM. It was *"Hola mamá."*

(HENRY re-enters.)

HENRY. And before that I was a one-cell swimmer.

DAD. You didn't swim. You were born here. *(HENRY sits.)*

HENRY. You don't understand, Dad. Can I play the game now? *(Long pause.)* Thanks. *(Sounds of Nintendo game. All stare at the screen.)* Where did you get the money for this?

MOM. He used some of the money for the telephone connection.

HENRY. Man, no phone? Messed up.

DAD. Not everything. I sold his bike.

HENRY. What? Mom!

DAD. What do you need a bike for? You're too old for it.

HENRY. How will I get around?

DAD. You have two feet.

HENRY. I can't believe this. Without asking me?

DAD. Respect me. Respect me. *(HENRY looks at him with so much anger he can't take it.)* In the ranch, we had nothing. And you cry for a bike? *(HENRY rushes out of the house. A long silence between MOM and DAD after HENRY goes. MOM has an understanding expression on her face even though she disapproves greatly of what DAD did. DAD looks at her and becomes a little boy. He is really not the*

pillar of strength he tries to be. Softening.) You know I
love him.

MOM. Then tell him.

DAD. Who told me? *(DAD goes to the Nintendo game and
starts playing. He glances at MOM several times. MOM
exits.)*

SCENE FOUR

*(HENRY is by himself in a field. OLIVERIO is watching
him from a distance. MOM approaches HENRY. OLIV-
ERIO disappears.)*

MOM. Henry.

HENRY. Mom.

MOM. Don't be angry with your father.

HENRY. I can't stand him.

MOM. Now God will punish you for saying that.

HENRY. We don't go to church.

MOM. I go. *(Pause.)* He's had a hard life.

HENRY. *I've* had a hard life.

MOM. I'll get your bike back.

HENRY. Forget it, Mom. I think I just saw some kid riding it
and he looked too happy.

MOM. You'll drive the car then.

HENRY. That piece of crap. I'd be embarrassed.

MOM. That's a way of life for a lot of people. There's nothing wrong with being poor.

HENRY. I want to be alone, Mom.

MOM. *No, you don't.* You don't want to be alone. No one
does.

HENRY. Yes, I do. *(MOM hesitates, then leaves quietly. HENRY sits there.)*

(Crossfade to DAD near a canal in the background. He sits there staring at the water. He looks across and sees GIRL smiling at him. She then disappears.)

DAD. Why did you go *hija*? I don't like being alone. *(Blackout.)*

SCENE FIVE

(DAD enters the house. He is covered with mud from the canal. MOM is trying to play Nintendo.)

DAD. I saw her.

MOM. You didn't see anybody.

DAD. I see her every time I clean out the canals. *(Silence. DAD is distraught again.)*

MOM. I don't know why I listened to you. No pictures, no talking about her. As if she was never alive. You even made me bury her far away.

DAD. I wanted her in Mexican soil.

MOM. This was once Mexican soil.

DAD. I have no worth here, so she couldn't stay.

MOM. Tell Henry about her now.

DAD. No. You know how I get. He'll think I'm weak.

(HENRY enters. DAD stares at him. HENRY eyes DAD's muddy appearance.)

HENRY. How come when I come in *that dirty,* I get in trouble? *(Silence. HENRY looks around.)* The silent treatment.

MOM. I'll get some towels. *(MOM exits. HENRY and DAD stare at each other.)*

HENRY. Hi, Pop.

DAD. Pop? What happened to papá?

HENRY. Yeah, what happened to you?

DAD. What do you got in that bag?

HENRY. Fish.

DAD. From where?

HENRY. The canal.

DAD. I told you not to go to the canals.

HENRY. Dad, this toxic waste could be dinner.

DAD. Don't go over there.

HENRY. Okay. I won't go there...*today.*

DAD. What did you say?

HENRY *(puts his Walkman headphones on).* Rap with me.

DAD. I'll rap your face. Stop that! *(HENRY keeps dancing.)* *¡Ya!* *(DAD grabs HENRY.)* I want you to say thank you for breaking my back for you. *¡Dilo!* For a roof over your head, for food on the table. Give me appreciation for all that I do for you!

HENRY. Is it Father's Day or something?

DAD. *¡Dilo!*

(MOM re-enters.)

MOM. *¡Dejalo!*

DAD. *¡Diga!*

HENRY. Thanks, *Dad.*

DAD. *¡Papá*

HENRY. Thanks, *Papá!*

DAD. The rest!

MOM. Stop it, you two.

HENRY. I know you work hard.

DAD. No, you don't. Your mother tells you.

MOM. Leave him alone. *(DAD lets go of HENRY. HENRY sits on the table and picks up a hardened tortilla. He breaks the tortilla.)*

HENRY. Look, I'm abusing a tortilla.

DAD. What did he say?

MOM. He's being funny.

DAD. Being funny while we work in the fields.

MOM. Get your father a beer.

HENRY. Gladly. *(HENRY puts his headphones back on to escape. He starts moving to the beat. He gets the beer from the refrigerator and continues dancing with a beer in hand, absentmindedly. MOM and DAD are unaware of his movement with the can of beer for they are talking quietly with each other. Then HENRY stops to adjust his headphones, and DAD looks up.)*

DAD. You have my beer?

HENRY. Here, Dad.

DAD *(correcting him)*. Papá. *(He opens the beer and it squirts all over his face. DAD runs after HENRY and catches him by the ear.)*

MOM. Stop it!

HENRY. OW! Dad, you're making a Van Gogh out of me.

DAD. Hear that! He told *me to go!* No respect!

HENRY *(breaks away). Van Gogh.* He lost an ear. Well, he cut it out.

MOM. Go out, Henry.

HENRY. Glad to. *(He exits to the bedroom.)*

DAD. He has no respect for me. The children born here are spoiled.

MOM. We came here to spoil our children.

DAD *(softens)*. Not like this.
MOM. You are jealous of your own son.

(HENRY enters and heads for the front door.)

HENRY. I don't need this.
MOM. Henry!
HENRY. What?!
MOM. Come back here.
HENRY. When you stop arguing!
MOM. Who's arguing? This is how we make love.
HENRY. Funny, Mom. I'm not in the mood.
MOM. Talk to your son! *Andale.*
DAD. You'll never do what I do. Never will you cut lettuce or pick from the trees, or anything.
HENRY. No problem!
DAD. *Understand? Understand!?*
HENRY. Who's going to pick the oranges in the tree out back? A wetback like you, Dad?

(DAD is about to reach for his belt when several BLUE MEXICAN PEASANTS [only seen by the audience] enter and restrain him. The PEASANTS finally let DAD go and they exit with HENRY.)

DAD *(softening)*. If I had all the money in the world, I would give that boy everything. I would give my wife the world. *(Pause.)*
MOM *(softly)*. Don't work in the canals, anymore. It brings bad memories to you. It turns you into this monster.
DAD. Sometimes, bad memories make the monster happy.

SCENE SIX

(Night time. Stars in the sky. OLIVERIO, a farmworker, stands in a field. White doves fly around him. He is smiling and enjoying the stars. He then starts shoveling dirt. HENRY walks by holding his ear. OLIVERIO notices.)

OLIVERIO. Something in your ear? Hey! I'm talking to you. Something in your ear like your finger? Then take your finger out.

HENRY. I thought it was bleeding.

OLIVERIO. *El corazon sangra... (Waits for a response.)* Only the heart bleeds, idiot.

HENRY. My Spanish isn't that good.

OLIVERIO. Pity. Where are you going?

HENRY. Nowhere.

OLIVERIO. Then you are in the right place.

HENRY. You work here?

OLIVERIO. I work all the time. And you?

HENRY. I don't work all the time. I'm too young.

OLIVERIO. I started working when I was this high. I had a rifle at the age of seven.

HENRY. To protect yourself?

OLIVERIO. To shoot my food. Jack rabbits. Sometimes a squirrel. Whatever came my way. I was sent off to herd the sheep and fend for myself. Sometimes it was months before I saw another person. Sometimes I forgot what I looked like. *No mirror in my pocket.* And I should have had one. I was very good-looking. Well, I needed to remind myself of that.

HENRY. You killed for your own food, at seven?

OLIVERIO. Or eight years old. I can't remember now. Once I ate a 'possum. It tasted very good. The tail wasn't good.

Felt like a snake in your mouth. The eyes were good. Well, when you are in the middle of nowhere and you are not sure you'll get a chance to kill for food again, everything tastes good.

HENRY. Would you eat 'possum again?

OLIVERIO. Eh, no...What's your name?

HENRY. Henry.

OLIVERIO. Mine's Oliverio. Like Oliver, but only better.

> *El señor de la tierra*
> *El señor de poesias*
> *El señor muy amable*
> *Con poesias mas allegres que tu.*

HENRY. What are you doing here?

OLIVERIO. Look at that. Don't you see it? Staring at the stars cleanses the soul. You should try it. Maybe it'll clean out that ear of yours. Look, there's the North Star.

HENRY. Great, I'm standing here with an old man that stares at stars.

OLIVERIO. And I'm standing with an idiot who holds his ear. I recognize that look on your face...Once, I picked up a lemon from the ground and put it in my pocket. It came from a man who was selling them. He saw the bulge in my pocket and rushed me to my father by the shirt collar. My father beat me up so much. Everyone saw him whipping me in the street. He wanted to teach me a lesson I would never forget.

HENRY. You didn't steal the lemon. You just picked it up.

OLIVERIO. And put it in my pocket. Same thing. My father was very determined I learn respect for the hard-working man.

HENRY. My father is a hard-working man. Hard at work in smacking me.

OLIVERIO. Maybe you deserved it.

HENRY. I didn't deserve that. Did you? *(Pause.)*

OLIVERIO. See that star. That one is mine. And that one over there. That one. That belongs to your family. Do you want a star to give away?

HENRY. A *what?*

OLIVERIO. Humor me.

HENRY. All right. Then, that one belongs to my girlfriend. Well, the one girl I really like.

OLIVERIO. Oh, you have a girlfriend. That's nice. Much too young to fall in love. Don't you know what love does to you? It makes you love more. It makes you hurt more. It makes you *horny.* Of course I've forgotten that part.

HENRY. *Que viejito.* What else do you have to amuse me, you old fart.

OLIVERIO. Fart? It was the dog. *(He smiles, then picks up some dirt and lets it sprinkle to the ground slowly.)* Look at this. This is my family. All of them. My uncles, my aunts, my father, mother, brothers, sisters, and my grandparents, and all the greats before them. But not the grandchildren or my wife. They are still alive and live well enough.

HENRY. Where are your children?

OLIVERIO. Lost. Like you.

HENRY. And the rest of the family is dirt?

OLIVERIO. The darker ones are mud. They're dust. Don't say dirt, sounds impersonal. Say dust. Say it like this, DUST.

HENRY. Okay, "DUST."

OLIVERIO. Dust. We are all simply dust. *Muchacho,* look at your shoes. You've been stepping on my mother. And that right there sticking to your pants, is one of my ancestors. She was an Aztec Indian. Okay. Take them home and introduce them to your family. *(HENRY starts to exit.) So soon?* Then go. But come back again.

HENRY. I should stay. I'll probably get my other ear smacked.

OLIVERIO *(looks at the stars)*. No you won't.

SCENE SEVEN

(BLUE MEXICAN PEASANTS enter. From their bags they take out tomatoes, onions, and some oranges and put them on the kitchen table. One PEASANT puts a carton of eggs and a package of tortillas by the stove. Another PEASANT opens one end of the tortilla package. Another goes to the shelf and gets the Mazola oil and sets it near the stove, and then picks up a dollar bill he knows is payment and puts it in his pocket. DAD enters and starts dicing up the ingredients for Migas. He tears a tortilla into bits and throws it in with the tomato and onion to fry. He then adds eggs.)

DAD *(while cooking happily)*. *Migas, migas, migas. Que sabrosas. Tomate, cebolla, y huevos. ¿Y que mas?*

(He looks into the refrigerator and pulls out a pan of beans to put in the mixture. GIRL appears. DAD accepts her presence.)

DAD. *Hija.*
GIRL. Hi, Daddy.
DAD. *Que bonita te miras.*
GIRL *(curtsies)*. Thank you, Daddy.
DAD. *Papá.* Remember what I told you. *Papá.*
GIRL. Okay, Daddy.

DAD. *¿Tienes hambre, mija?*

GIRL. Yes, Daddy.

DAD. *Diga, si papá.*

GIRL. *Si, papá.*

DAD. *Muy bien. Tengo migas. Que sabrosas. ¿Te gustan? Huelelas.*

GIRL. Smells good, Daddy.

DAD *(correcting her.) Papá.*

GIRL. *Daddy.*

DAD. *Si, mona.*

GIRL. I want to take my bike out. Can I borrow your keys?

DAD. Keeyz?

GIRL. Yeah. The keys. I need the keys to take my bike out of the shed. You locked it in there. So I want the keys.

DAD. The keeyz?

GIRL. Yeah. The keys.

DAD. Okay. *(DAD puckers up and makes a smoochy kiss noise.)* There.

GIRL. No, not a kiss, the keys.

DAD. Oh, I thought you said a keeyz.

GIRL. You do that all the time. Okay, *las llaves. Presteme las llaves.*

DAD. *Mejor. Aqui estan. (He takes the keys out of his pocket.) ¿Otra cosa?*

GIRL. Can I have a quarter?

DAD. Me no speak English.

GIRL. Daddy!

DAD. *Cuando hablas Español.*

(GIRL exits as HENRY enters.)

HENRY. Hey, Dad. I want to borrow the car. Can I borrow the keys?

DAD. Keeyz?

HENRY. Yeah. I want to see my friends over at the high school. I won't be long.

DAD. Yule want the keeyz?

HENRY. Yeah. That's what I said. Can I have the keys?

DAD. Okay. *(Dad puckers up to make a smoochy kiss noise.)*

HENRY. Oh, Dad! Not a kiss, the keys!

DAD. OH!...No.

HENRY. Ah, come on. There's going to be a pep rally.

DAD. A what?

HENRY. A pep rally. Cheerleaders will be there.

DAD. Girls?

HENRY. Yeah.

DAD *(thinks)*. You go.

HENRY. The keys, Dad. You sold my bike.

DAD. All right. One hour.

HENRY. One hour! That's not enough.

DAD. Then give me back the keeyz.

HENRY. Man...What can I do to stay out a bit longer? Get you a beer?

DAD. Respect me.

HENRY. I do, Dad.

DAD. No you don't. You don't know what it means.

HENRY. *Por favor*.

DAD. Go for an hour and a half.

HENRY. Dad, listen. It's exciting. There's dancing, Music. Everyone is happy. It's fun, Dad. Want to go?

DAD. Me? No. You go. Go for two hours. Maybe three.

HENRY. *Gracias papá.*

DAD. You should learn Spanish. It's good for you. If you forget the language, you'll be lost. You'll never know yourself, or your history.

HENRY. *No hablo español.*

DAD. *¡Vete!*

HENRY *(laughing). Adios, Papá.*

DAD *(long moment later, under his breath).* Go kill yourself.
   (Slow blackout.)

SCENE EIGHT

*(DAD and MOM are sitting at the table with bills and
statements scattered about. MOM does the bill paying as
DAD watches. Then MOM puts money in an envelope and
that in a zip-lock bag. She then puts it in a secret place: a
hole in the wall under the sink.)*

DAD. My friend's children speak the language so beautifully.
   I understand them. They have respect. I don't understand
   Enrique.

MOM. Henry will do better with—

DAD *(overlapping on "better").* Enrigue.

MOM. Henry.

DAD *(pause).* Mothers and sons always stick together and
   gang up on the father.

MOM. Why don't you go to school and learn English yourself? That's the secret to success.

DAD. Why waste my time? I'm going to die in Mexico.

MOM. You're not going back.

DAD. Yes, I am. I have to be buried in the soil that speaks
   my language. If I don't, then I'll truly feel like a foreigner.

MOM. You don't feel anything when you are dead.

DAD. *I* will.

MOM *(pause).* You want that boy to succeed, you let him
   speak the language of this country. You'll see that I am
   right. The schools here—

DAD *(overlapping on "here")*. Help families lose their children. He talks to me about things I don't know. Like pepto, pepto bees-mo.

MOM. What?

DAD. He invited me to go to the school for the pepto-algo. I don't know. The girls, cheerleaders.

MOM. Oh, the pep rally.

DAD. Yes. How did you know that's what it's called?

MOM. If we both take a class, we would learn English very well. And you would understand your son better.

DAD. Take a class to understand my son? I refuse to be made an idiot in public.

MOM. It's a school. You go there because you are an idiot. *(DAD looks at her. Long moment. Softly.)* Do you like Salinas better?

DAD. In Salinas I can forget about her. Here, I think I see her all the time.

MOM. Try to forget. Then the misery will leave you. *(MOM exits. DAD sits silently. A blue arm opens the kitchen window and slips several school books onto the sink counter. Moments later DAD takes one of the books and tries to read it. He covers one eye in an attempt to better see the page. He then puts the book down and exits.)*

SCENE NINE

(Near a canal HENRY is assembling a fishing pole. DAD enters.)

HENRY. Dad. Ah, there's a bunch of fish in there. I saw them swimming. I borrowed the fishing pole and...Are you mad?

DAD. What are you doing here?

HENRY. Fishing?

DAD. *¿Como?*

HENRY. With a fishing pole.

DAD. Ah. You don't need a fishing pole. In the ranch, all you needed was some line and a hook. *Mira.* I'll show you. Get this fishing line and wrap it around something. A rock, or a little stick. Then put a hook at the end. *Aqui.* Now put it in the water. This end with the stick, you put in your pocket, but first twist the middle of the line around the button of your *camisa. Asi.* When you feel your shirt moving, you got a fish.

HENRY. You can catch a fish that way?

DAD. *Pescados grandes.*

HENRY. Get out of town. You won't catch a thing.

DAD. *Vamos aver. (DAD waits for the fish. Suddenly, his shirt tugs and a fish splashes up.)*

HENRY. I don't believe it

DAD. Watch it. Watch it. Aye. You let it get away! *Bueno.* That's what it's all about.

HENRY. That's totally amazing. I've never seen anything like that. Cool. So utterly cool.

(GIRL appears from across the canal. DAD's mood becomes somber.)

HENRY. Let's do it again over here. Kind of embarrassing in a way, but who cares. We're catching fish. Dad, let's... Dad? What's the matter? Dad? Papa? Hey. Come on. Don't stop, now. This is the best fun we've had in a long time. Dad? *(DAD is staring at GIRL smiling at him. HENRY can't see GIRL.)*

DAD *(slowly).* I miss Mexico.

HENRY. Dad. It's not too far.

DAD. *Vamanos.*

HENRY. Dad. Geesh. *(Under his breath.)* Man, get it together. *(DAD exits. GIRL watches HENRY gather the fishing gear and start to go.)*

SCENE TEN

(MOM is listening to a "Learn The English Language" tape.)

TAPE. I am hungry.

MOM. I am hungree.

TAPE. I am hungry.

MOM. I am hungry.

TAPE. Repeat. I am hungry.

MOM. Repeat I am hungry.

TAPE. What would you like to eat?

MOM. Apple pie and coffee.

TAPE. I am not hungry.

(HENRY enters.)

HENRY. Mom.

MOM. Sh!

TAPE. I am not hungry.

HENRY. Mom.

MOM *(turns off the tape).* I'm practicing my English. You're bothering me. Making me nervous.

HENRY. You speak good enough.

MOM. Oh no. People stare at me when I talk. I have to get rid of the accent.

HENRY. It's all right, Mom.

MOM. I want to speak properly. No accents.

HENRY. Mom, even in the English language there are different accents.

MOM. That's not true.

HENRY. Yes, it is.

MOM. Well, then, it all sounds the same to me.

HENRY. But it isn't. Listen to me. Here's one accent. *(Southern California accent.)* Killer dude. Totally awesome. Freakster. And here's another one. *(Boston accent.)* Where's da ca? Or this. *(Chicago south-sider accent.)* Hey, I'a breaka your face.

MOM. It all sounds the same to me.

HENRY. Ma. I'm sure it's like that over there. Regional Spanish?

MOM. Well, yes. Different accents. But I liked the first one. I'll speak like that. That accent sounded good.

HENRY. The California talking?

MOM. Keeler doode. I like that. What does that mean?

HENRY. Nothing.

MOM. How can something mean nothing?

HENRY. Put the tape away.

MOM. No. I want to be educated. *You can be educated.*

HENRY. I have enough skills to make it in life.

MOM. That's not good enough. Go to college.

HENRY. We've talked about this before and you said you'd stop. I want to rap.

MOM. Then go rap and I'll study. *(Pause.)* You're stubborn like your father.

HENRY. Where is he?

MOM. He went his way and I went mine. *Hombre tan sonso.*

HENRY. Most would leave, Mom.

MOM. I can't leave my husband. I'm Catholic. Besides, we were taught not to leave a man if he has some good in him. Anyway, I have to help him.

HENRY. Help him do what?

MOM. *Nada.*

HENRY. What's wrong with him? Is he sick?

MOM. No. Go rap.

HENRY. What's the matter then?

MOM. I have to listen to my tape. Go. I'll study for the both of us.

HENRY. Mom. I'm old enough to know what's going on.

MOM. No, you're not. *(Pause.)* Go. You are making this hard on me.

HENRY. Sure. I don't want to be a burden. *(HENRY exits. MOM sits there quietly for a long moment. She then turns on the tape.)*

TAPE RECORDER *(MOM's voice).* Everyone is a burden. Even memory becomes a burden. The memory of it brings you down. Tears you to pieces. Best to forget and remember only when you are alone. If the mind was more powerful you could tell it to erase things. Then record a different message over it. And play what you want to hear again and again.

TAPE. I am thirsty.

MOM. I am thirstee.

TAPE. I am thirsty. Repeat.

MOM. Repeat.

(MOM turns off the recorder, but it still continues. We hear "repeat, repeat, repeat" in a strange way for a while longer. Then the "repeat" fades away. MOM walks over to a shoe box. Inside the shoe box are several ruffled hair ribbons that belonged to GIRL. There is also a small

*school picture of GIRL. MOM stares at the picture. She
then goes to the refrigerator. As she opens the door, a
BLUE MEXICAN PEASANT's face is inside and looks out.
MOM takes a beer and closes the refrigerator door. She
then takes some paper out of the shoe box and walks over
to the trash can. As she is ready to toss the paper, a blue
arm reaches out of the trash can and takes the paper, then
crumbles it and disappears into the trash can with it. Moments later MOM goes to the sink and slices a lime. Outside of the window are several BLUE MEXICAN PEAS-
ANTS looking miserable. They stare at MOM. She doesn't
see them. She goes to the table and squeezes the lime slice
into the beer. She continues to look at the picture. She licks
her side wrist, sprinkles salt on it and licks the salt off. She
then drinks her beer. A group of BLUE MEXICAN PEAS-
ANTS enter and surround her. They have devastated looks
on their faces. MOM continues looking at the picture. She
starts to cry and the PEASANTS back off. MOM quickly
regains control of herself, and the PEASANTS approach
again. They stare at her as if to tell her something, but
then give up and exit. Crossfade to darkness.)*

SCENE ELEVEN

*(GIRL is at the window. She opens it and looks in. Mo-
ments later HENRY walks past and exits. A bit later, DAD
enters, gets his boots, and exits. MOM enters and sits at
the table to sew a dress.)*

GIRL. Mommy. Mommy, can you hear me? Mommy!
Mommy, why don't you open the door? I was out there

and you didn't even hear me. Where did Dad go? He can hear me. You're too busy to hear me. Daddy always hears me. He really listens when I speak Spanish. What are you doing? Mommy! I'm talking to you. I know, I know, you're too busy. *(Pause.)* Why do you and Daddy fight? It's no good to fight. Why do you let him be mean to my brother? You're not mean. *(Pause.)* Mommy, don't go to Salinas without me again. I have to stay here all by myself when you go. I get scared. I get so scared. Mommy, you never listen to me. Listen to me. Listen to me. I hate you. I hate you. *(MOM starts to cry.)* I'm sorry, Mommy. Don't cry. I'll be good. I'll be quiet. I'll go outside to play. I'm so sorry. *(MOM stops crying. GIRL feels better. Crossfade.*

SCENE TWELVE

(DAD enters with a few cantaloupes in his arms. He puts them down and turns on the radio and hears rap music. He quickly changes it to a Spanish radio station. He listens for a moment and then slices a cantaloupe. MOM enters.)

DAD. *Aye querida.*
MOM. You're in a good mood.
DAD. I am. Look. I want to talk to you. Have some of this.
MOM. What is it?
DAD. Melon!
MOM. I know. What do you want to tell me?
DAD. Guess.
MOM. You quit smoking.
DAD. No.
MOM. Well, you should. You stink up the house.

DAD. Guess again.

MOM. You quit drinking.

DAD. NO.

MOM. Then it's not good news.

DAD. I got a job.

MOM. You got a job?

DAD. A better one than the fields.

MOM. Is that why you left so early?

DAD. I had to.

MOM. They were asking me where you were. I told them you were urinating. You still didn't come back so I told them you had infection on your *"pito."* [Pronounced peet-to]

DAD. Why did you tell them that?

MOM. I had to.

DAD. Anyway, I did go to urinate, then I saw Julio.

MOM. Julio!?

DAD. He's starting a business.

MOM *(suspicious). What kind of business?*

DAD. A restaurant. He wants me to be a partner.

MOM. He wants you to put all the money in. You know I don't trust him.

DAD. Neither do I, but it's a chance.

MOM. A chance for what? To lose what you already have?

DAD. What do I have? I have nothing. How can I lose nothing? The Salvadorians are taking the field work from us. They do the work for practically nothing. Soon they'll be doing all the work. There's so many of them who are trying to survive like us.

MOM. What are you going to do in that restaurant, wash dishes?

DAD. I did that before. This time, I get to be in charge. I'll be the boss. If I only give Julio money today to—

MOM *(overlapping on "money")*. We have no money.

DAD. We have some hidden.

MOM. That's not ours.

DAD. We'll use a little and then replace it.

MOM. It's not ours. We're giving it to Henry when he decides to go to college.

DAD. It came from our suffering. Think about our future. He will benefit from it.

MOM. I didn't come to this country to steal from my child.

DAD. He doesn't know he has it. He's not serious about school. He won't be for a long time and by that time, I'll have replaced it two times over.

MOM. No. My son means more to me than that stupid restaurant.

DAD *(overlapping on "than")*. Than me?

MOM. Than that restaurant.

DAD. What about me? What about me? *(Long tension-filled silence. DAD goes to the shoe box. He throws out the contents and holds a picture of GIRL.)* Do it for her!

MOM. Julio will make you eat dirt.

DAD. Give it to me.

MOM. He's not doing anything for you. Only for himself.

DAD. It's a chance!...It's a chance. Listen to me, *querida*. We have to work together the way the Koreans do. You know when they come to this country they have nothing. Just like us, nothing. Then all the members of the family put their money together and buy one store. They all work it, bumping into each other, day and night, saving all the profits, until they pay for the store. Then they buy another store, and together work that one until they have enough to buy another one, then another one, then another one. Finally, all the members who put their money in for the first store, get their own store at the end. They do this all the time. That's how they have all the grocery stores. And we're grateful for at least they are selling tortillas.

MOM *(pause)*. None of those Koreans went into partnership with Julio. It's with their own families they do such things. No one cheats a family member and if they do, the whole family tells him to go to hell.

DAD. My family is all over and they are more miserable than me! That is why I am going to use the money with Julio.

MOM. No, you're not.

DAD. Yes, I am.

MOM. No, you're not.

DAD. *Querida.* This time you are wrong.

MOM. Our son is our only chance for self respect.

DAD. Because I didn't give it to you?

MOM. We are immigrants to this country. I didn't come with high expectations. It's foolish to have—

DAD *(overlapping on "foolish")*. Foolish to have high expectations of this country, or me?

MOM. Not with my son's college money.

DAD. Then with what? *(MOM covers her ears to avoid listening. DAD looks at her wedding ring. She notices this, and after a long moment slips off the ring and gives it to DAD. DAD then starts to exit.)* You are a strong woman for doing this. *(Pause.)* Julio also thanks you. *(He exits.)*

MOM. Julio is a *pinche cabron.* And so are you.

SCENE THIRTEEN

(OLIVERIO is pushing a wheelbarrow across the field. DAD walks by holding a plastic bag with money inside.)

OLIVERIO. *Estrellas, estrellas, estrellas. Muchas estrellas.*

(HENRY comes on and sneaks up to scare OLIVERIO.)

OLIVERIO. *Ep-pa.*

HENRY. Scared you.

OLIVERIO. Scared me like a ghost.

HENRY. I got good news. Remember that girl I told you about?

OLIVERIO. No.

HENRY. Yeah, you remember, old man. She's going to Mesa College. It's a good way to get the hell out of here if you got the money.

OLIVERIO. Those *gringos* like to use Spanish names for everything now. One time, everything here was named in Spanish. They changed them to English, and now back to Spanish to sell it as high real estate. Hal-ci-en-da Heights, ugh. La Play-zza di May-yo, ehh. Yor-ba Lin-da. *Es yerba linda.* Such a travesty to corrupt a beautiful language. At least their gardeners say the names correctly. Ah! A beautiful night. Oh, look. Isn't that beautiful? Let's see how smart you are. What is it?

HENRY. A star.

OLIVERIO. What is it really?

HENRY. A meteorite?

OLIVERIO. No. It's a mass with gas. That's what we are. And, we are all the same. Should be no names, no labels, no political affiliation. All those things make war. Understand? *(No answer.)* Someday you will. *(They see a falling star.)* See that one going down?....Has a lot of gas. Too many tacos. *(HENRY's not amused.)* What's the matter? Life can be fought with a smile and a little joking. For that matter, death. When you're my age, you won't care about too many things. Too much effort. Will give you ulcers. *(Burps.)*

HENRY. How old are you?

OLIVERIO. Why do you want to know? Isn't it enough to see the gray hair and the wrinkles running into each other? *(Smiles.)* Did you know that the tears of the clown are so true.

HENRY. What?

OLIVERIO. He cries.

> There's tears painted on his face, but he cries.
> He cries from what he feels inside.
> *"Las lagrimas"*
> It's painted on the face
> But he smiles
> Do you know why he smiles?...
> He smiles because he learned that he has to face a
>   situation, with the opposite.

(No response.) I've learned that true wisdom comes with death. *(No response.)* Your girlfriend is going to college? Go yourself. Maybe what I learned in the fields someone with a degree can teach you.

HENRY. Money problems, *hombre*. Plus why should I? Where's it going to take me?

OLIVERIO. At least to show that some dirt can mix with the white sand. Look, my boy, someday you'll find that money doesn't make you happy. It's the work. If you like what you do, then you'll care less about the money and the things you can get with it.

HENRY. That's what you're trying to tell me? My parents are picking for me? Give me a break.

OLIVERIO. No. They're picking for everybody.

(HENRY looks at OLIVERIO for a long moment, then exits. At that moment, GIRL appears. OLIVERIO sees GIRL and goes to her.)

OLIVERIO. Are you ready?

GIRL. In English?

OLIVERIO. Will you interrupt?

GIRL. I don't know.

OLIVERIO. You always do. All right. Ready?
>   In the eyes of a child.

GIRL. The child sees so much.

OLIVERIO. Rainbows never pass without mention.

GIRL. Ooohh. I liked that one.

OLIVERIO. The face brightens
>   in peaceful acknowledgment of the colors
>   The cheeks of a child
>   soft, soft
>   soft pillows of joy
>   When pressed against a parent's face
>   Brings more colors of happiness
>   and even more joy.

GIRL. Can I sing?

OLIVERIO. And from the tenderness of the lips
>   A voice so pure exists
>   Making all who have saddened
>   A temporary haven
>   One that will only continue
>   If you insist
>   The baby cries
>   And sounds so demanding
>   Deciding quickly what the child needs

GIRL *(interrupts on "child")*.
>   I have a little brother. His name is Enrigue.
>   That's what my father said was his name.
>   I told you, teacher. Enrigue. His name is Enrigue.
>   She said, "Henry. His name is Henry."
>   Your name is Henry.

OLIVERIO. He needs everything. Mother, father, soil,
    all the tools to begin.

GIRL. I'm going to teach him English. So they don't make
    fun of him. He'll be good in school, like me.

OLIVERIO. Pity those who don't understand.

*(OLIVERIO exits as a group of BLUE MEXICAN PEAS-
ANTS enter and sit around GIRL.)*

GIRL. Okay everyone. Are you ready? Itzy bitzy spider, went
    up the water spout. Down came the rain and washed the
    spider out.

*(The PEASANTS then gently grab GIRL. As she goes limp,
they toss her in the movement of water going through an
irrigation canal. In this stylized dance of "water rushing"
they exit with GIRL. DAD enters and runs toward them. He
doesn't reach GIRL in time.)*

DAD. ¡HIJA!

SCENE FOURTEEN

*(Lights up on HENRY. He is watching DAD in the dis-
tance. They are both being watched by the BLUE MEXI-
CAN PEASANTS. DAD drops to his knees. Crossfade to
OLIVERIO and HENRY.)*

HENRY. You like to pick?

OLIVERIO. I like the life on the farm.

HENRY. It's degrading.

OLIVERIO. To you maybe, but to me, it's wonderful. Seeing how God makes a seed grow from a soil that is black like hell.

HENRY. It's hell, all right.

OLIVERIO. Feeling the sun that can silently peel your skin from its intense rays.

HENRY. I only tan on a beach.

OLIVERIO. From water that comes all the way from the mountains in the north, then through these canals. Canals that hold life. They can also hold death. Are you afraid to die?

HENRY. No.

OLIVERIO. Death is a blanket. It stops life, yet it's the beginning of something else. Go home now. Your parents need you.

HENRY. Maybe I will go away. Just leave with twenty cents in my pocket and make a life.

OLIVERIO. Sounds familiar.

HENRY. My dad said he did that.

OLIVERIO. I had ten cents in my pocket. Will you follow your father's footsteps?

HENRY. What do you think?

OLIVERIO. I think you made up your mind. Go then.

HENRY (hesitates). I will.

OLIVERIO. Get what you need for the road, but travel light. Good luck.

HENRY. I'm going. Don't rush me.

OLIVERIO. What kind of work will you find?

HENRY. What do you mean, what kind of work?

OLIVERIO. You have to survive. I worked in the fields for money to pay for food. Don't tell me you have an American Express card?

HENRY. I'll rap.

OLIVERIO *(confused)*. How much they pay you?

HENRY. Thousands of dollars if you're good. That's the profession I want. I want to feel important.

OLIVERIO. The oldest profession in the world is just as important.

HENRY. The oldest profession in the world?

OLIVERIO. Without it, there would be no population.

HENRY. The oldest profession in the world is—

OLIVERIO. Farming. That's the oldest profession in the world. Think about it.

HENRY. I will. *(HENRY walks to his own home. DAD is there waiting for him.)*

DAD. Enrigue. I'll need your help in the restaurant.

HENRY. What restaurant?

MOM. Your father bought a partnership with Julio.

HENRY. He's a drunk, Dad.

DAD. I'll be running the business. You work as a busboy.

HENRY. No way.

DAD. *¿Por que no?*

HENRY *(hesitates)*. 'Cause, I'm going to school.

DAD. What school?

HENRY. The junior college. Mesa College.

MOM. I want you to go to the state college.

DAD. You're not even serious about life. How are you going to go?

HENRY. What if I get a scholarship?

MOM. This is wonderful. I knew it. Henry, I want to show you something. Oh, your father and I worked hard for this. We've managed to scrape some money together for you. I've been sewing for ladies to add to it. I hope you'll appreciate it. We obligated ourselves to save it for you. So your life would be better. It's not that much, but at least you can pay for a few classes, books and—*(As she speaks she reaches for the envelope in the hole. The BLUE MEXI-CAN PEASANTS look through the window. MOM doesn't find the zip-lock bag with the envelope of money. She turns to DAD.)* You took it!

DAD. Julio needed more. I had to do it. No more dirt on my fingers. No more getting my hands moist from the *"canales de muerte."* You know how I hate working *los canales,* as well as the fields.

MOM. He's our only hope.

DAD. What about me? You're married to me, not to him.

MOM. You took the money that belonged to him. *(HENRY runs out. OLIVERIO catches him and they embrace.)*

DAD. Everything that comes into this house is mine. I can do whatever I want with it. *(MOM and DAD stare at each other as the lights turn blue, then they exit.)*

(The BLUE MEXICAN PEASANTS enter wearing skull masks. They strip the house of all its furniture. They place a microwave in the room. "Itzy Bitzy Spider" is heard faintly in the distance.)

END OF ACT ONE

ACT TWO

SCENE ONE

(The room is bare. There is a microwave in the kitchen. MOM is chopping oranges in strong strokes that patterns her anger.)

HENRY. Mom. Mom. Have you used the microwave? I was lucky. I won it at the school raffle. I never win anything and I got it. I wanted the bike, but the microwave was the second prize. You can cook tortillas in it. *(DAD is cursing in the other room.)* What's his problem? *(No answer.)* You two keep things from me. I wish I had a sibling to team up with me against you two. *Sibling.* What a funny word. Sounds like a chicken.

MOM *(stunned, then threatens to strike)*. I'm going to break your mouth.

HENRY. Why? What I do?

MOM. Get out of my sight, you snake in the grass. *(About to strike HENRY but he grabs her arm.)*

HENRY. I'm not a snake! Call me anything, but that.

MOM. Oh, my God. I'm turning into your father.

HENRY. Some kind of compulsion. Beat the kid.

MOM. Enrigue. He stopped it, didn't he? I told him NO MORE OF THAT BEHAVIOR. *(HENRY starts rapping with sound effects.)*

(DAD enters.)

DAD. *Que esta pasando aqui. Tu sabes que no me gusta rap.*

MOM *(exploding)*. You said Julio knew what to do.

DAD. He had the place rented for two months.

MOM. He strings people along.

HENRY. How much did Julio take you for?

MOM. Even your own son knows about Julio.

HENRY. Everyone knows about Julio. He stands in front of the school waiting to gyp someone. If he thinks you got something, he goes after you. When I was coming home with the microwave, he tried to give me a ring for it. I told him to get lost.

MOM. Did you see the ring?

HENRY. No. He said he had it in a safe place.

DAD. Why didn't you tell me this before?

HENRY. Because you never asked. *(Silence. HENRY then goes to the refrigerator and gets three beers. He gives one to MOM and DAD, and one for himself. He pops open his beer. Slow blackout.)*

SCENE TWO

(In the fields. A glimmer of stars. The BLUE MEXICAN PEASANTS walk across holding baskets of fruit, a baby bundle, and a television set. A somber MOM follows them with the shoe box. They exit. Much later, OLIVERIO enters to see the stars. HENRY then enters. He sees OLIVERIO, but wants to walk past, avoiding him.)

OLIVERIO. Where are you coming from and where are you going? Come on. Relax. Soon life will be over and all that has preoccupied you will not be that important anymore.

Ignoring me? Fine. Then I'll talk to myself. I'll make up a poem right here as you walk away.

El espiritu te envia
El corazon se enternece
La vida se va
Sin todos los muebles.

HENRY. What does that mean?

OLIVERIO. How the hell should I know?

HENRY. But you said it.

OLIVERIO. I only speak from the heart. A lot of times I don't know what it means.

HENRY. That doesn't make sense.

OLIVERIO. Oh, but it does. It's much later when I figure them out. But by that time, it's too late. I've already lost the original feeling of the poem and feel something else. Then there comes a new poem, and I have to figure that out, too. It gets to be too much, but I write a lot of poems that way. I meant it. Where are you going?

HENRY. I don't know. I have to get away.

OLIVERIO. From what?

HENRY. From everything. From my parents. I'm going crazy with them. I don't know who they are or what they want from me. You know, I don't always understand the way they talk. How come they don't talk like you?

OLIVERIO. Poetry?

HENRY. No. In simple English so I can understand. I get bits and pieces and I know I miss the rest. They know too, but say nothing.

OLIVERIO. Henry. Language doesn't mean a thing. It's what's here, in the heart, that speaks. *(Long moment.)* There's your girlfriend's star. Have you seen her lately?

HENRY. Yeah. She made me mad by touching my arm. So I hit her.

OLIVERIO. Oh, boy. You're a handful. Why I got you, I'll never know.

HENRY. What?

OLIVERIO. Look at that star.

HENRY. I have no more stars to look at.

OLIVERIO. Then look at the moon. The moon looks so innocent, and at times it realizes it's not. So it goes away for a while to think things out. And then it returns to try again. Each time it fails, but it keeps coming back to try again. A new poem.

> *La luna no sabe*
> *Como todos la miran*
> *Ella siempre va y viene*
> *Para que todos la admiran.*

HENRY. What the hell does that mean?

OLIVERIO. I just recite them, I don't explain them. Anyway, if I did tell you, it would lose its mystery. It's not what the words mean. It's how the language makes you feel. If you feel the meaning, then why do you need to know the words?

HENRY. Because, if you don't know the words, you get hit.

OLIVERIO. There's meaning even behind that. Don't always listen to the sounds of the whip. Feel the meaning behind it.

HENRY. I'll never understand you, or them!

OLIVERIO. You will always think about us. Even when you are far away. Even if you run away up here, you'll think about us. See those stars. You think about them even when you don't see them, especially on those foggy nights. You'll think, "Where are the stars? I know they are there." Another poem.

> *¿Donde estan las estrellas?*
> *Los guiero con toda mi alma*
> *Brillan orgullosas*
> *Aun cuando nos dormimos.* (HENRY exits.)

Where are the stars
I love them, will all my life
They shine with pride
Even when we sleep.

Boy, that sounds like shit in English.

(With some passion.)
Cuando ellas brillan
Mi tristeza resultan
Y mis lagrimas caen
Quiero decirle a mi gente
Que no se vayan muy lejos
Y siempre recuerdan
de las mañanitas allegres.

SCENE THREE

(HENRY is at the kitchen table doing his homework. DAD enters and stands there, staring at him.)

HENRY. Dad, I have homework to do. *(No response. Still more staring.)* Dad, leave me alone. I'm doing *tarea.*

DAD. *Tarea. ¡Digalo bien!*

HENRY. *Tengo ser me tarea. Adesso.*

DAD. *Adesso? Eso es Italiano.*

HENRY. I like Italian. And for your information, that's where I'll go if I'm going to travel. There, or Egypt. See, I already know about Mexico.

DAD. No, you don't. I thought I knew everything about the United States, and when I came here, I was mistaken. Where's your mother?

HENRY. She went to class.

DAD. I told her not to go.

HENRY. Give her a break.

DAD. She's planning to leave me. *(Long pause.)* In this house, *vamos hablar puro Español, des de ahora.*

HENRY. Speak in Spanish only? Not in your life.

DAD. You're going to write your homework in Spanish. And if you don't, out you go.

HENRY. I'll go! *(HENRY gets up, but DAD grabs him and throws him on the chair.)* I'll fail if I write this in Spanish.

DAD. I failed, too! *Comiensa su tarea en español.*

HENRY. Dad!

DAD. *¡En este momento! ¡Andale!* (DAD pushes HENRY off the chair.)

HENRY. Go to hell!

(DAD pulls out his belt. A BLUE MEXICAN PEASANT appears. He is holding a belt and watches the action.)

DAD. *Venga aqui. Lloron.* You baby.

HENRY. Baby? I saw you near the canal crying! *Crying.* You are a grown man who cries near the canal! Macho, macho, macho.

DAD. I'm going to kill you.

HENRY. Go ahead and do it! It just doesn't hurt me anymore!

DAD. If your mother could hear you talking to me in this way.

HENRY. If I told her you never stopped, she'd leave you! And you would be *solo! Muy solo!*

DAD. So you think I'm an animal?

HENRY. No, Dad. I think you're crazy. *(DAD is about to strike HENRY, but HENRY protects himself by picking up a basket of laundry and throwing it towards DAD.)*

DAD. You run from *su papá*, and I'll beat you harder.

HENRY. *¡Tu no eres mi papá!*

DAD. *Venga aqui.*

HENRY. No. You're going to hit me.

DAD. I'll hit you harder if you don't come *en este momento.*

HENRY. You'll hit me anyway. *(DAD stares at HENRY for a long time. HENRY weakens to DAD's authority. He approaches DAD, stops, and turns around to get hit.)*

DAD. I'll kill you.

HENRY. Go ahead. Being dead is better than this.

DAD. *En Español.*

HENRY. No.

(DAD raises the belt and at the top, freezes. Other BLUE MEXICAN PEASANTS appear and start swinging belts in slow motion during HENRY's monologue. HENRY will be stoic as he speaks, staring straight out.)

HENRY. See, Dad. It was bound to happen. I got used to it. I got used to all the beatings. Ever wonder if that would happen? This is not how you get respect. If only I had brothers and sisters to share in this delightful activity. If only they'd been here to either take it with me, or help me in telling you how wrong you are in doing this. Ever since I was little I had to cover what you did to me. I had to have a smile on my face and pretend nothing happened. So no one would suspect. Never see my shame. Never let anyone know what happens in this house. Keep hitting me, Dad, if it makes you feel better. After all, this is your house. I am a snake in the grass for not understanding you. For being too young and stupid to know why you hurt. I will always remember the beatings with pity for you, because the scars of this, will be a lot deeper for you.

DAD *(unfreezes).* ¡LLORA! ¡LLORA! *(As he unfreezes, the PEASANTS stop whipping the air. They express silent pain. DAD ends his swing.)* Ya. You will respect your father. *(HENRY exits. DAD stands there staring at the belt for a long time. He then goes to the refrigerator for a beer.)*

(Mexican waltz music as GIRL enters. DAD sees her and they come together to dance. DAD is enjoying his dance with his daughter. They continue dancing on the next lines.)

GIRL. *Papi.*

DAD. *Si, mija.*

GIRL. Love me?

DAD. With all my heart.

GIRL. Love Enrigue?

DAD *(breaks down). Si. (They continue dancing. Then GIRL stops and exits. DAD calls out, softly.)* No! Come back. Come back to me! *(Sobbing.) Aye, hija.* Why do you keep leaving me? Why did you go? I miss you so much. I missed you when I was at work. I missed you when you started to grow from a baby. You were so independent. Strong like your mother. Nothing could hurt you. Then you started to mistreat me by learning a language I couldn't understand. You came home to sing songs that had no meaning to me. I couldn't understand. In my own home. I couldn't understand your voice. I couldn't learn. I was too busy in the fields. You don't talk to anyone when you work the fields. You have no time. As each day passed, you became a stranger to me. I gave you life. *(Attempting to be in control.)* It would have been nice if you said a few words in *español* before you...Forgive me for punishing you on the day you died. I will never lose that guilt.

(DAD sees MOM and HENRY in a light in the background. HENRY is covered with large bruises.)

DAD. I hit him only because I needed to make a man out of him. It's true, Henry. *(MOM takes a breath.)* I'm preparing him for what will happen out there. *(Lights fade out on MOM and HENRY.)* Is everyone leaving me? Is everyone leaving this man who has nothing? Nothing but misery? You think the devil is me? I'll wrestle with the devil. I'll take him by the neck and force him to get away from me. At night, he comes and tells me what a failure I am. I wake up and see that he is right.

(BLUE MEXICAN PEASANTS enter. They are wearing hideous masks. The one wearing the devil mask coaxes DAD to fight with him.)

DAD. I drink so I'd be too drunk to go with you. I know why you do this to me. No matter how foolish my decisions are, I'm a good man, and you can't stand that. *(Pause.)* It's not my fault. This is what I was taught. To make them good. She didn't listen to me, and dirtied her dress. The dress her mother and I worked so hard to buy. I hit her for dirtying her dress. She ran to the canal to wash it, and then, she fell. She ended up washing her dress with tears. And my tears have never stopped. *(Slow blackout.)*

SCENE FOUR

(HENRY has the rap music very loud, and is on the furniture dancing to it. The BLUE MEXICAN PEASANTS are dancing, too. MOM enters after a few moments, not too surprised at his acting out his frustration. She's frustrated too. The PEASANTS exit.)

MOM. Henry, get down.

HENRY. No.

MOM. Don't punish me, get down. *(He won't.)* Henry. Henry. *Henry*!

HENRY *(with the rap)*. I'm black and blue. I'm black and blue.

MOM. Stop it.

HENRY. Don't you get it, Mom? It's an English expression.

MOM. Stop it.

HENRY. You just don't get it. I'm black and blue!

MOM *(turns off the music)*. Stop it, Enrique.

HENRY. No, I'm E.B.J.

MOM. No, you are my son and I want you to sit down. I want to explain something to you.

HENRY. Explain what to me? Why I get beat?

MOM. Henry! He only gets this way when he's frustrated.

HENRY. I'm frustrated. I'm suffering here worse than that tearful Madonna. And what have you done? Stand there while it was happening. You closed your eyes, Mom, and I can't forgive you.

MOM. I didn't close my eyes. I told him to stop.

HENRY. He didn't, Mom.

MOM. He said he would.

HENRY. He didn't.

MOM. Then why didn't you tell me?

HENRY. Because I thought I loved you.

MOM. *Henry!*

HENRY. WHAT?

MOM *(losing her temper.)* Don't talk to me like that. Don't you talk to me like that. I'm your mother. You don't know what I do for you. Both of you blaming me!? I'm stuck between two stubborn boys who are fighting. Don't you think I get tired of this? Do you think I'm made of stone? Don't you see how I mourn for the way you two behave? I'm sick and tired of going between you and your father. Never appreciation from the two of you. You think I'm on your father's side when I ask you to have pity for him. He thinks I'm on your side when I ask him to let you be a teenager. It is impossible to be both judge and lawyer. The two of you have been spoiled by my understanding attitude. Let me make this clear today and at this moment. I'm finished with protecting you both from each other. At this point, I could care less if you kill each other. Go ahead. I don't have a family. I lost it a long time ago. I have animals living in here and I've had it! *(She exits.)*

HENRY *(starts rapping sounds).* Now you know, Now you know, Now you know, Why I'm black and blue. *(Ends with rapping sounds.)*

SCENE FIVE

(HENRY is in the field rapping. OLIVERIO hears him and goes to him.)

HENRY. Yo.
> And my name is Eee
> E.B. Jay
> I'm here to find the only way

To tell you who, who I really am
But first,
I'm no fool
Stop messing with my mind
Or I'll give you a fight
Yo
Word to your mother. Olé.

OLIVERIO. *Dios mio.* If this is poetry, I'm getting out of town.

HENRY. I am. As soon as I get my act together, I'm gone. *Hasta la vista.* Word to your mother.

OLIVERIO. You're stepping on her. If you need help with your poetry, you knew I was here.

HENRY. I need no help from you.

OLIVERIO. What is E.B.J? Sounds like some disease you get from mosquitos. You need help with the words. Right now, it sounds like you put them together with spit. I put the words together with dust.

HENRY. Stop with the dust business. I'm bored of it. All right?

OLIVERIO. So you want to be a poet.

HENRY. A rapper.

OLIVERIO. A clapper?

HENRY. A RAP-PER. Get out of here, man.

OLIVERIO. Your verse stinks.

HENRY. Go away.

OLIVERIO. What's the first line?

HENRY. What?

OLIVERIO. To that ugly thing you were singing.

HENRY. Damn. I think I said "yo."

OLIVERIO. Yo?

HENRY. Yo. It's not Spanish.

OLIVERIO. What does it mean?

HENRY. It's how you say it.

OLIVERIO. *Las palabras dicen mucho.*

HENRY. What are you doing?

OLIVERIO. *Pero lo que dicen, no es todo la verdad.*

HENRY *(translating reluctantly)*. The words say a lot. But it's not what they say that is, that is, happening.

OLIVERIO. *Cuando me siento mal.*

HENRY *(more into it)*. But when I feel very sad.

OLIVERIO. *Necessito su paciencia.*

HENRY. All I really want is your patience. Patience? Shit, when I'm black and blue.

OLIVERIO. People share their hopes and pains. That's part of life. Don't expect things to change so fast. Unnatural when it does. Are you going to be a clapper?

HENRY. You mean a rap-per? I don't know.

OLIVERIO *(picks up a clump of grass)*. You got to be patient. Sometimes the plant takes its time. Other times, the weeds choke it. But the plant still sucks water from the ground, pollinates, and feeds the people. That's a beautiful plant for you. Look. A worm is hiding in between the roots. Get out, little fellow. Find another place to rest your body. Then come back and nourish the soil. Go. Go churn the ground with your friends so it's ready for the seeds.

HENRY. A bird is going to eat that worm.

OLIVERIO. It has to take his chances.

HENRY *(pause)*. Maybe he needs a star.

(OLIVERIO disappears and MOM enters. She gives HENRY the picture of GIRL.)

MOM. Go to your father. He's finally ready to explain her to you. *(HENRY looks at the picture then at MOM. He exits.)*

SCENE SIX

(HENRY enters and sees DAD. HENRY is outraged. He holds out the picture of GIRL. DAD drops his head in pain.)

HENRY. Who is she, Dad? *(DAD won't look at the picture.)* WHO IS SHE? She's someone you're ashamed of? Someone you've been hiding? I get it. I get the whole picture. It comes as a shock, Dad, but I should have figured it out. You had a child from some other woman, and the guilt has been eating you up inside. *(DAD is silent. He is almost suffocating with grief.)* Come on! Come on!

(DAD won't move. He is frozen. Finally HENRY pulls out his belt and is about to smack DAD with it when the BLUE MEXICAN PEASANTS enter, wagging their index fingers and shaking their heads "no." GIRL enters. Her eyes meet DAD's.)

GIRL. Daddy?

DAD. *Mija. (GIRL exits.)* NO!!!!

HENRY. WHO IS SHE? *(DAD looks all around and can't find GIRL. In desperation, he grabs the picture and then looks at HENRY holding the belt. They look at each other for a long time, then DAD turns away. HENRY drops the belt after seeing the look in DAD's eyes.)*

DAD *(softly)*. If you ever want to kill me, I give you permission. Why would I want to live anyway? I'm no good. I hurt the people I love. I can't give you a better life. I am ashamed of myself at every turn. I make mistakes every single day. This picture is the next most beautiful thing to your mother. I never wanted to tell you about this because I didn't want you to suffer like me...*(Pause.)* You and your mother have a connection I envy. We wanted two children. A son for her and a daughter for me. We had made plans to spoil each one in our own private way. Then she went away...I had the love of a daughter and she went away. She is your sister. One year after you were born, she was taken away from me. From your mother and I. I have not been able to forget her. Do you know what kind of pain is in your stomach when you see a child you've given life to sink to the bottom of the water?...No. You don't understand my pain. No one does. Your mother is a strong woman and she let God have her fifteen years ago. But I couldn't let her go. I want to hold her every day. I want to touch her hair and the ruffles on her dress. I DIDN'T GET A CHANCE TO LOVE HER...To think she would have been married by now. *(HENRY has been retreating.)* I blame myself. I am a stupid man...Come back here with your belt and *dame shingasos*. I deserve it for what I have done to you. I let misery take me away. This house and the one in Salinas have had misery imprinted on the walls. It's time to wash it away. *(Silence.)*

HENRY. Dad. You have a son left. *(They hesitate, then hug.)*

SCENE SEVEN

(In darkness, rap music is playing loudly. Light on a sofa chair. DAD is sitting there listening to the rap music. The expression on his face alternates from: Rap isn't too bad, I'll give it a chance, It's okay, There's some good in it, etc. HENRY enters, wearing glasses and holding a book bag.)

HENRY. Dad? Dad! You like that?

DAD *(nods his head with the beat, then).* I like it. I like rap. Spanish, English, whatever. *(HENRY smiles as he watches DAD's head nod up and down with the beat. He starts to exit and passes MOM. MOM has huge pieces of paper stuffed in her ears. HENRY waves to her and she waves back smiling. He exits.)*

SCENE EIGHT

(OLIVERIO is in the field staring at the stars. HENRY enters.)

HENRY. Hey.

OLIVERIO. Hello.

HENRY. Where've you been?

OLIVERIO. Where've *you* been?

HENRY. No place. Just doing a little studying, and...Hanging out with my dad. Can you believe it?

OLIVERIO. What about the clapping?

HENRY. Rapping? Nothing...I came to tell you that—

OLIVERIO *(overlapping on "you").* I already know. *(HENRY smiles and turns to leave.)* You ever get a chance, stop at a field that is about to get picked. Look at all the vegetables and tell them you respect them. Then, come and watch the pickers, and tell them you respect them. Doing those two things is like thanking the guy above.

HENRY. I came to say—

OLIVERIO. Goodbye? I already said goodbye.

HENRY. You did?

OLIVERIO. You say goodbye everyday.

   To the dust. To the stars,

HENRY. To the moon...
    To the worms.
    To the vegetables
        picked by my father and mother
    Their sweat
        to give us fruit to eat
    Their sacrifice
    For the love of their son
    Their dreams
    A small step
        towards happiness.

OLIVERIO. Not bad. *(Challenging.)*
    Children of the dust

HENRY. Following the crops of their parent's frown

OLIVERIO. Families canvassing the land of land

HENRY. Walking across patches of striped earth

OLIVERIO. Green, beige and brown

HENRY. Heavy boots, callused hands

OLIVERIO. Machetes swinging on tough plants

HENRY. Children watching parents work
    From the trailers with broken doors.

OLIVERIO. Very nice. I like how you say it.

HENRY. Oliverio, where do you live?

OLIVERIO. I live nowhere, and I live here on the field.

HENRY. How poetic.

OLIVERIO. "Yo." You better believe it.

(OLIVERIO smiles and waves goodbye to HENRY. HENRY turns to go home. The BLUE MEXICAN PEASANTS enter. They smile and walk up to OLIVERIO.)

OLIVERIO. You don't have to force me to go with you. I've known you all my life. I only do what I can to change the pain. So I laugh as you all finally smile.

(GIRL appears.)

OLIVERIO. And I hold the hand of the most precious gift there is. The love of a child. *(OLIVERIO and GIRL exit.)*

(HENRY enters his home and sees MOM and DAD in the kitchen. DAD hands HENRY an envelope filled with money.)

DAD. For your school.
MOM *(sing-song)*. Julio will kill you for it.
DAD. I would kill for my family.
MOM. What about the ring? *(DAD shakes his head.)* Julio is a crook.
DAD. Julio's a crook.
HENRY. I can't take the money. I'll work for it myself.
MOM. Take the money, before your father spends it again.
HENRY. I'd even work in the fields for extra money. It would be good for me, so I'd respect.
DAD. No. You saw your parents pick, you have enough to be humble about.
HENRY. *La luna no sabe*
     Como todos la miren
     Ella siempre va y viene
     Para que todos la admiren.
     (MOM and DAD stare at HENRY.)
MOM. Where did you learn that?
HENRY. It's one of Oliverio's poems.
MOM. Whose poems?

DAD. *Era de Oliverio.*

MOM *(to DAD)*. What does this mean?

HENRY. He doesn't explain them. He only recites them. *(HENRY smiles, then looks out the window.)* Hey. Look at the stars. Aren't they beautiful. Mind if I go outside and take a look? Come out and see them with me. *(HENRY goes out the door. He looks up at the stars. There is a sense of hope. MOM and DAD stare at each other for a long moment, in bewilderment.)*

DAD. Oliverio used to recite them when he was....*alive.*

MOM. It can't be. He rolled over in the tractor fifteen years ago. He's dead.

DAD. Yes, but the spirit never dies.

MOM. We must tell Henry. *(DAD smiles and is about to shake his head "no" when a blackout occurs.)*

END OF PLAY

CHARACTER NOTES

HENRY: Rambunctious, attempts to lighten even the gloomiest of moments. Uses rap for tension release.

OLIVERIO SANTOS: Loves poetry. Passionate about nature. His words are loaded with meaning. He is humorous and never didactic.

DAD: Buried in his misery. He is a good man, but constantly fails in his attempts for betterment. A good heart, but not sophisticated. Tormented by memories. His lack of English understanding causes friction with his very American teen-age son.

MOM: A good mediator. Quick witted. Extremely adaptable. Has plans for self-betterment.

GIRL: She wears white ribbons and her dress is filled with ruffles. Spunky girl. A father's joy.

MEXICAN PEASANTS: They have blue skin, and gray, bluish clothes.